Jessica's Dog, Cody

Copyright 2024
Liz Ciufo

Jessica's Dog, Cody

ISBN: 978-1-7355521-4-9
eISBN: 978-1-7355521-5-6

No part of this publication may be reproduced, distributed, or transmitted in any form or by any means, including photocopying, recording, or other electronic or mechanical methods without the prior written permission of the author, except in the case of brief quotations embodied in critical reviews and certain other noncommercial uses permitted by copyright law.

Editor: Kerri Yund

Printed in the United States

Jessica's Dog, CODY

by
LIZ CIUFO

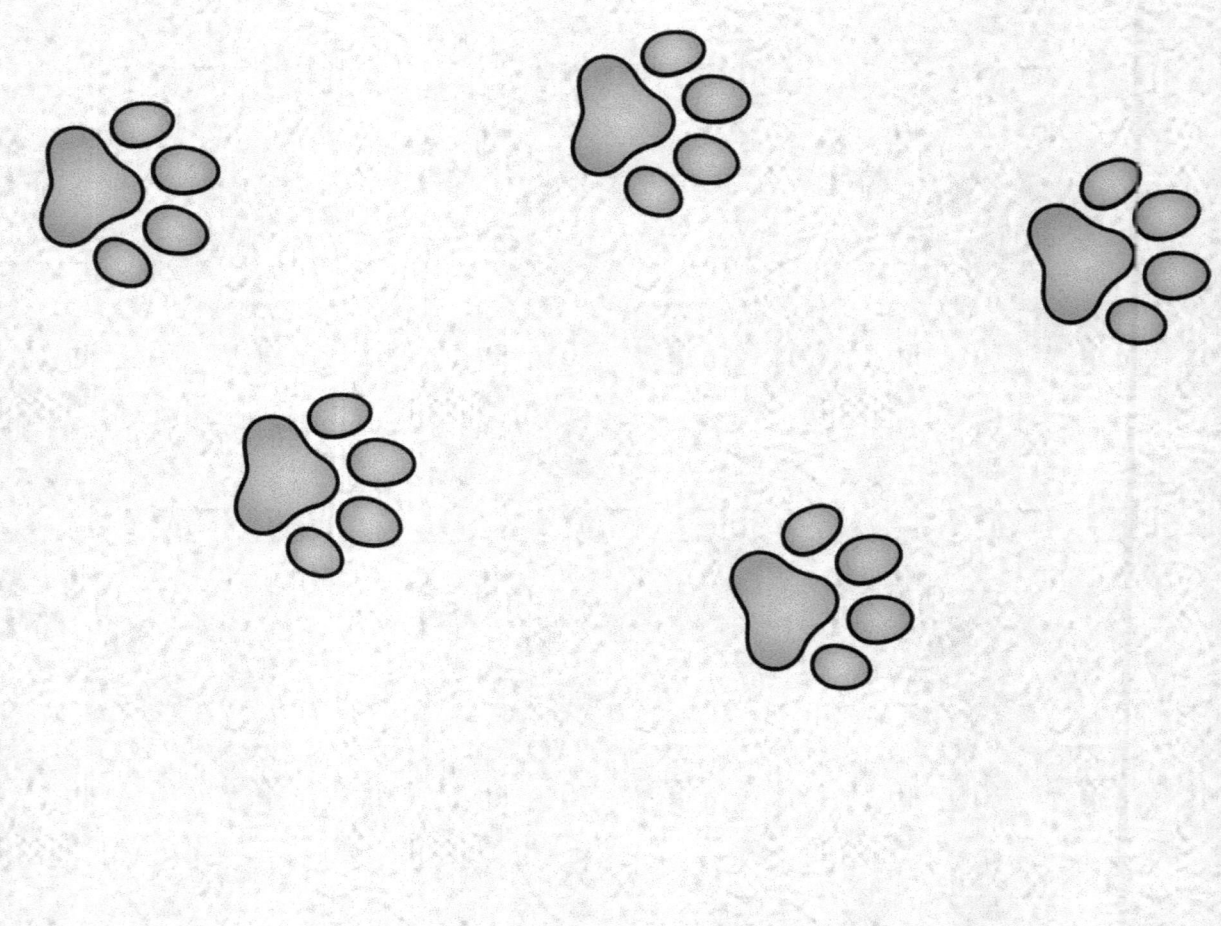

 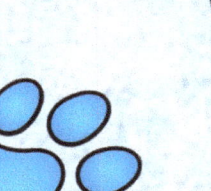  

This book is dedicated to the Placer SPCA in Roseville, California, and to all its devoted staff and volunteers, both past and present. Their hard work and unrelenting love and care for every shelter animal that comes through their facility is uplifting and inspiring.

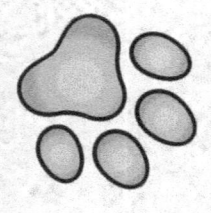
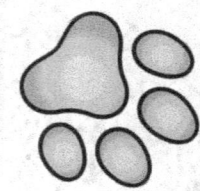
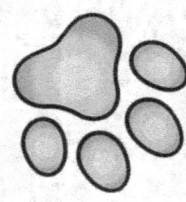
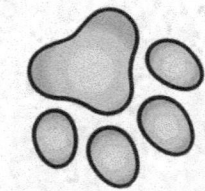
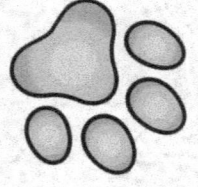
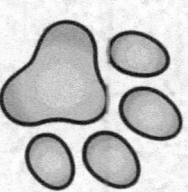
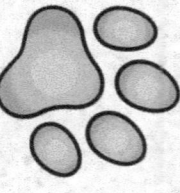

FOREWORD

Over 25 years ago I volunteered at a local animal shelter. It was through that experience that I realized my true passion and left my career in law enforcement to begin work in animal welfare. I now have the privilege of serving as the Chief Executive Officer at the Placer SPCA in Roseville, California.

Founded in 1973, the Placer Society for the Prevention of Cruelty to Animals (Placer SPCA) is the largest and most comprehensive non-profit animal welfare provider in Placer County — one of the fastest growing counties in California, serving almost 400,000 residents.

The mission of the Placer SPCA is to enhance the lives of companion animals and support the human-animal bond. We do this by working to ensure a number of things: that every adoptable companion animal in Placer County has a home; that every lost companion animal in Placer County is reunited with its owner; that every dog and cat owner in Placer County has access to affordable spay and neuter services; and, that every companion animal is treated with kindness and respect. None of these things would be possible without the countless hours of hard work and dedication of our nearly 800 volunteers.

The contributions of our volunteers to the overall care and well-being of homeless animals in our community is unmatched. From socializing cats or taking dogs on walks, to fostering bottle baby kittens, cleaning habitats, or working special fundraising events, we depend on volunteers like Jessica for the daily care of our animals.

Jessica was part of our Junior Volunteer Team program where youth ages 13 – 17 (alongside a parent or legal guardian) help animals in need by assisting in the everyday care and socialization of our animals.

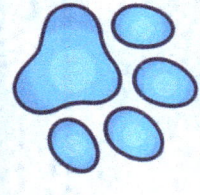
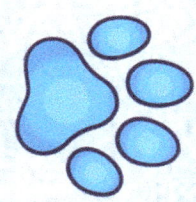

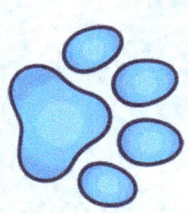

In addition to volunteering as a Junior Team, our Humane Education programs offer a variety of ways for youth of all ages to get involved. One of these programs is our Youth for Animals Club which helps kids ages 9 – 13 understand how they can make a difference in the lives of animals. In this club, they learn about animal welfare organizations (how and why animals enter shelters and how to care for them in shelter environments), proper care and treatment of animals in general (safe handling, nutrition, exercise, grooming and health, and responsible pet ownership), and explore careers in animal welfare. Another program for kids ages 7 – 12 includes our summer Animal Camps. During these camps, children learn about responsibility, kindness and respect for animals and all living things.

Just as Jessica did, at the Placer SPCA we know that no matter how young, kids can make a difference!

Leilani Fratis
Chief Executive Officer,
Placer SPCA, Roseville, CA

*Please note, some programs are temporarily on hold at the current time. Additionally, training and procedures change from time to time. Please consult the Placer SPCA website at https://placerspca.org for current procedures and volunteer opportunities or call them directly at (916) 782-7722 for the most updated information.

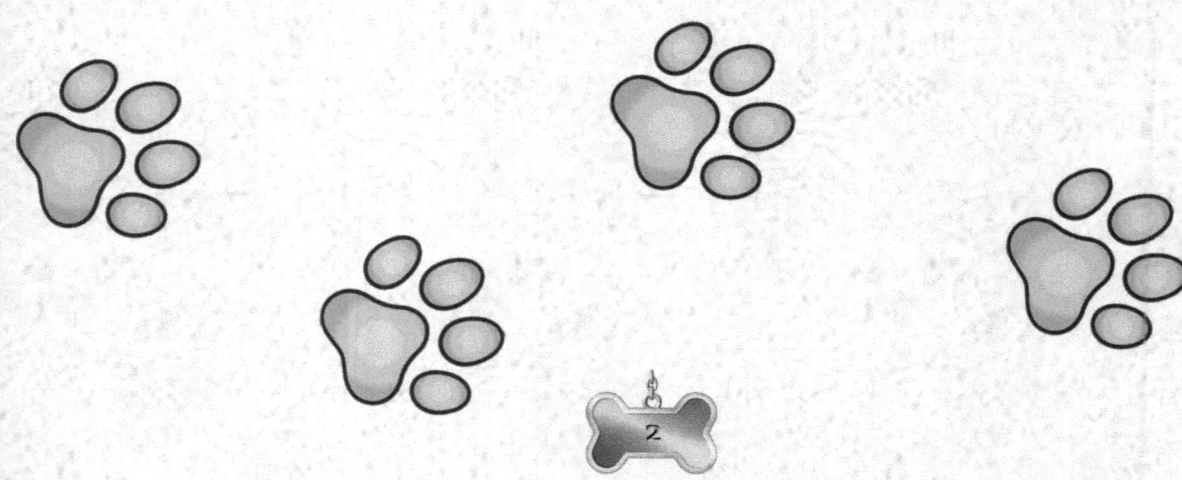

INTRODUCTION

This is the second book in a series highlighting how kids can make a difference in their world.

The first book in the series, *Skip's Dog, Lola*, is about Jessica volunteering at an organization that rescued and trained large-breed dogs as assistance dogs for military veterans. Read that book to see the special dog Jessica fell in love with and the impact she made on her corner of the world. It is available on Amazon.

In this book, *Jessica's Dog, Cody*, Jessica volunteers again at a local animal shelter, and falls in love with another special dog. To see what happens, turn the page and read on!

Do you know a child who is making a difference in their world? How can you make a difference in your world?

  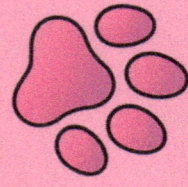

Hi, my name is Jessica. This is a story about how I came to love (and keep) a dog named Cody.

My little Nugget!

When I was growing up, my dad was in the military, so we moved around a lot. During that time I lived all over the country – in Georgia, Alabama, Florida, North Carolina, New Mexico, Virginia, Florida again, and finally, Washington, D.C. When I was 15 years old, my dad retired from the military and we moved one final time to California. I was looking forward to settling down in one place and having a permanent home.

US Air Force Band Concert
Constitution Hall

Lovin' the hotel life!

When we first moved to California, we lived in an extended-stay hotel for a long time while we were looking for our perfect, forever home. My twin brother, Josh, and I were homeschooled, so we did school right there in the hotel room! We were 16 years old and just starting eleventh grade.

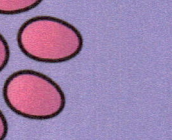

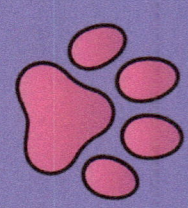

Because we were homeschooled, we got to learn in lots of different ways. Sometimes we studied out of books and did lessons on the computer. We also studied about foreign countries and then got to visit them, learning the geography, politics, culture, food, and customs.

Blarney Castle, Ireland

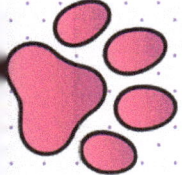

Another important way we learned was by working in areas that interested us, either getting paid jobs, or volunteering. For example, my brother started his own business making and selling paracord bracelets that were popular with kids and hikers; and I took care of my neighbors' pets when they went on vacation.

Since I love dogs and thought I might want to be a dog trainer when I grew up, my mom and I looked around for a place where I could learn more about dog care and volunteer to help from time to time. We found an organization called the Placer Society for the Prevention of Cruelty to Animals (abbreviated SPCA), in Roseville, California.

 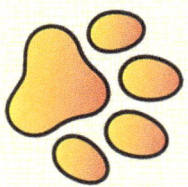 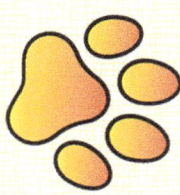 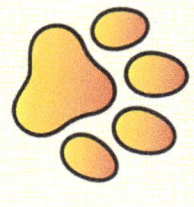

The Placer SPCA is a non-profit organization but also serves as the city shelter (or kennel) for lost, abandoned, or abused animals. It is also a place where people can bring their pets if they are no longer able to take care of them, like if an elderly person moves out of their home and into a care facility.

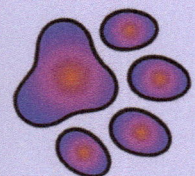
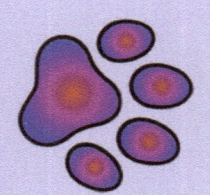
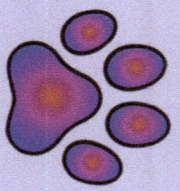

Meghan,
Shelter Operations Manager

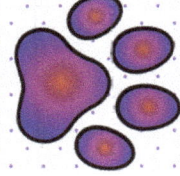
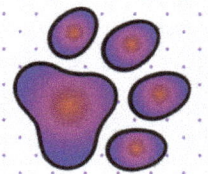
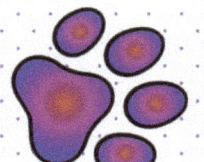

Lots of dogs to love!

You can volunteer there once you turn 13 years old as part of what is called a "Junior Team." A Junior Team is made up of a kid who is 13 – 17 years old, working alongside a parent or legal guardian. My mom agreed to volunteer with me, so I could not wait to sign up for the training!

Bunnies need love too!

My mom and I were required to do A LOT of training there before we could begin working with the animals. First, we had an introduction class telling us how the SPCA works. Then we took classes to teach us how volunteers care for the dogs, cats, and other critters like bunnies. This class taught us how to "socialize" or hang out with the animals, giving them attention from outside the cages.

From outside the cages, we would do things like approach the animals from the front of the cage, talk some sweet talk to them, and let them sniff our hands through the cages. We could also give them some treats through the bars of the cages to get them used to coming forward when someone came to their cage. We had to be careful not to look the dogs in the eye just in case they found it threatening. Stray dogs and dogs who have been hurt in the past are often untrusting of humans. But they can learn that most humans are kind and bring them good things, like tasty treats!

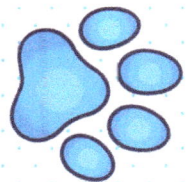

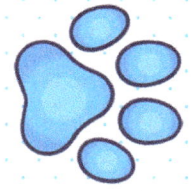

So many cuties

After that, we took more advanced classes for dogs. These classes taught us how to enter and exit kennels safely, and how to interact directly with the animals without them feeling threatened. We also learned how to do some basic obedience training, teaching them to follow simple commands, and learned how to take the animals on potty walks. Later, we took separate training classes for cats and critters (like rabbits, guinea pigs and hamsters), but chose to work primarily with the dogs because that is what I love best!

Two furry friends

One of the main goals of the Placer SPCA is to get stray animals adopted out to forever, or, in this case, "fur-ever," homes. Many stray dogs are afraid of people or may have bad habits that make people not want them in their homes. So, one of the key jobs of volunteers is to spend time with the animals, getting them to trust a person who is talking to them, petting them, or giving them treats. Another key job is to teach the animals polite behavior so they will be better pets in people's homes.

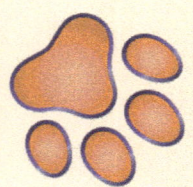
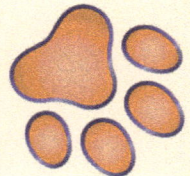

My tiger-striped friend

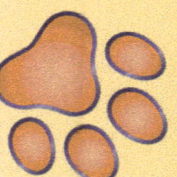
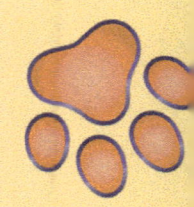

Going into kennels to pet and play with dogs was especially fun, and I fell in love over and over with many different pups! There were tiger-striped dogs, black dogs, white dogs, furry dogs, short-haired dogs, small dogs, big dogs, old dogs, puppies, three-legged dogs, one-eyed dogs — and I loved them all! We were also encouraged to teach the dogs a few basic tricks like "leave it" and "take it" to help with impulse control, or "sit" and "stay" and other basic commands.

After volunteering for a few months, and taking all the required training, my mom and I were able to walk the dogs outside the cages for potty breaks and for exercise. We took them to enclosed yards where we could throw balls for them and have more room to run around. We worked several times a week and over time my volunteer hours began to stack up.

It's fun outside!

About a year later, after we finally moved from the hotel into our own home, and I had done over 100 hours of volunteering, the SPCA got in a stray, pregnant dog who had a litter of six puppies in the shelter that very night! We saw the puppies when they were just two days old and bumbling around with their eyes still closed. Did you know that puppies don't open their eyes until they are one to two weeks old? They were so adorable when they were piled in a big heap, fast asleep!

Puppy love!

When the puppies were six weeks old, the SPCA decided to give two puppies each to three different foster families away from the shelter until they were ready for adoption at eight weeks old. Fostering meant taking care of the puppies in place of their mother and giving the dogs a taste of what it would be like to live in a real family home. This meant we could work on potty training, more socialization, and more training, while also giving them a break from the stressful and sometimes noisy shelter.

Two puppies to love!

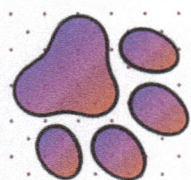

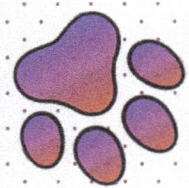

Well, that's all I needed to hear! My mom and I immediately took the Foster Care Class and brought home two fat, squirmy puppies! One puppy was feisty and caramel colored with a few white patches. She was a girl we named Sophie. The boy was a little butterball of a puppy with tan fur and some black accents, along with some white underneath his chin. We named him Cody and immediately fell in love!

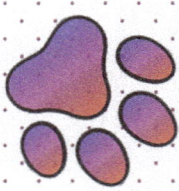

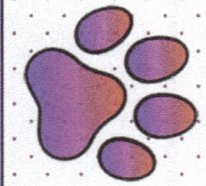

Cody & Sophie

Sleeping beauties

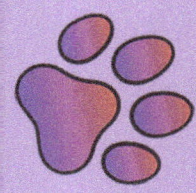
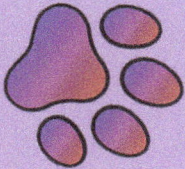
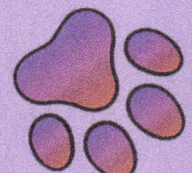

Cody was quite mellow and let his sister wrestle and play with him. Sophie was so small she fit under the bars on our coffee table and would hide under there teasing Cody by reaching out her paw and yipping at him. It drove Cody crazy since he was a little too chubby to get underneath! When it was time for them to return to the SPCA to be adopted, I made these advertisements, which described their sweet personalities perfectly.

Cody

Cody is an eight-week-old, rough and tumble, mixed breed pup with lots of personality. He loves exploring the yard and has probably eaten a little something from every corner of it. Speaking of eating, he loves his chow, especially if he's stealing it from his sister. She is also his favorite plaything and chew toy, but he does love his stuffed toys and Nylabone, and is learning to chase a ball. He is adventurous and independent and is happiest going for a good romp in the yard. He is learning to do his "business" outside, and sometimes comes when called. He is still getting familiar with his name. Every day he gets more coordinated and is growing like a weed. He's a loveable, fun pup with lots of energy!

Sophie

Sophie is a mischievous, spunky, eight-week-old, mixed-breed pup. She is adventurous and inquisitive and loves exploring the yard and romping around in the grass. She is learning to do her "business" outside and sometimes comes when called. Sophie is all sweetness — when she's asleep! When she gets in trouble, she has perfected the innocent face just in time to make you fall in love with her all over again. She is

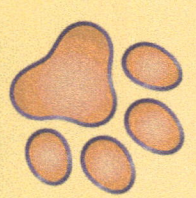
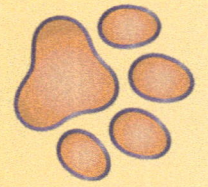

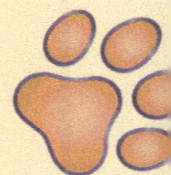
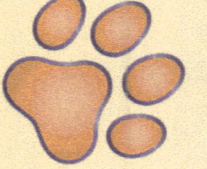

energetic and loves chasing her brother, Cody, around. She has personality in spades and energy to match. She's a good eater and is growing by leaps and bounds. She will steal your heart — and your shoes!

 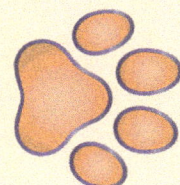 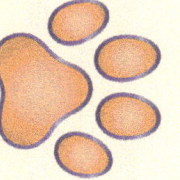 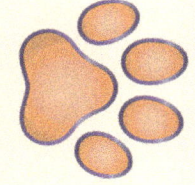

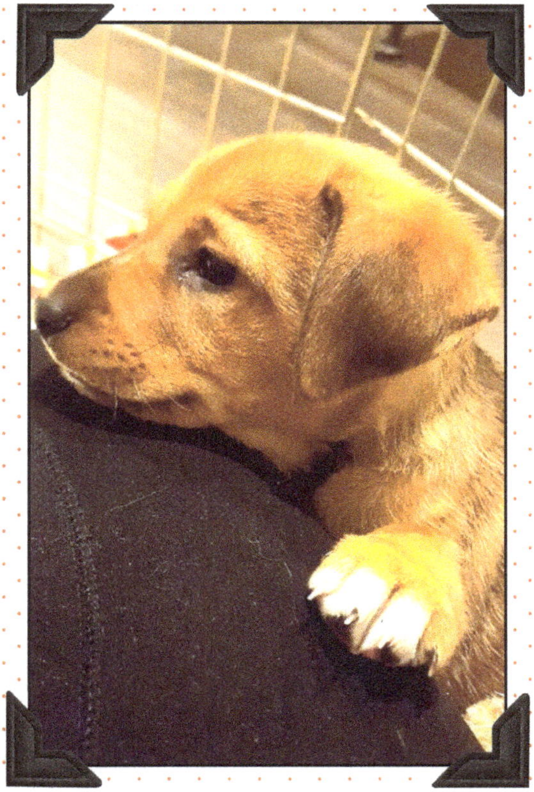

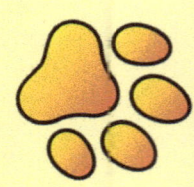

Trying to say goodbye

I don't know what makes you fall in love with one dog over another, but we fell in love with Cody. We knew we would have to take him back to the kennel at the end of our two weeks with him and that he would get adopted the very next day — puppies always do. In fact, whenever there are puppies up for adoption, there's usually a line of people outside waiting for the SPCA to open!

At the time, we didn't have a dog of our own and were not planning to get one yet, so, with great sadness, we took Cody and Sophie back to the SPCA the day before they were supposed to get adopted. The next day, we went to the SPCA an hour before they opened to snuggle with Cody and Sophie one last time, and to see the rest of the puppies in the litter. I was so sad I thought I was going to cry at the thought of some other family taking my Cody home.

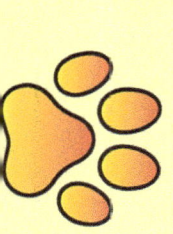

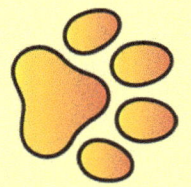

Remember the story of how I fell in love with a dog named Lola (*Skip's Dog, Lola*), then had to give her up to a military Veteran who needed her as his Assistance Dog? Well, here I was again, in love with a dog, I mean, really in love, and about to give him up to someone else – AGAIN! As I cuddled Cody closely, I looked pleadingly at Mom sitting on the floor across the kennel from me, and her soft eyes looked back at me. An unspoken decision floated on the air between us. She said, "Should I go tell the staff that we're adopting him?" I nodded, "Yes", with tears of joy in my eyes.

Only minutes after my mom had finished the paperwork to adopt Cody the adoption floor opened, and people flooded to the kennel where the puppies and I were. A young man, holding the hand of a cute little girl with bouncy pigtails, knelt beside the door, gestured to Cody in my arms, and asked if he was available. "I'm sorry," I said. "He's not available. He already has a forever home."

  # EPILOG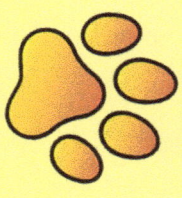

Now, years later, Cody is still the love of my life! He is a friendly, energetic dog who is descended mostly from working breed dogs. Since we moved from the farm, Cody no longer has sheep to herd or animals to guard. But he loves going on walks, meeting other dogs, and lazing about in the sun in our back yard. He gives lots of good cuddles, and I can't imagine our family or our home without him.

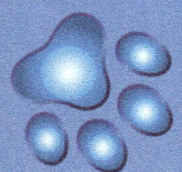
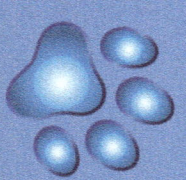

Amazing volunteers!

The Placer SPCA in Roseville (or another local shelter) is a wonderful place to get excellent training with animals, and practical work experience in a place that serves the community in a meaningful way. You can learn animal care and basic training, how to follow the rules of an organization to keep yourself and the animals safe, how to work with other volunteers as part of a team, and how to record walks and socialization time. But most importantly, you can learn what it feels like to serve others and make a difference in your world!

Altogether I logged about 150 volunteer hours at the SPCA. They have other programs like summer camps for kids there as well, so check them out on the web at https://placerspca.org/. There are also many other rescue and shelter organizations that can always use volunteers. And remember — you are never too young to make a difference somewhere!

AUTHOR'S NOTE
FOR PARENTS AND TEACHERS

Instilling a heart of volunteerism in children is so important — a spirt of giving of themselves, of generosity, and of serving others. The inspiration for that can come from parents and family members, caregivers, teachers, spiritual leaders, or other important people in a child's life.

There are many ways to instill this attitude in children, but I think the most important is to model it yourself. Working alongside my daughter at the SPCA wasn't always what I wanted to do, but I knew how important it was for her to have the opportunity to serve there. It ended up being a blessing in my life as well, as I cared for animals in unfortunate situations, and gained appreciation for, and inspiration from, the dedicated and hard-working volunteers and staff, including my own daughter! To watch people choosing to make a difference every day is inspiring.

Here are some ideas for instilling a heart for serving and volunteering:

1. **First and foremost, lead by example.** When your child sees you serving others, they learn the importance of generosity of spirit without a word being said. Almost everyone has something to give, from small gestures like taking cookies to the fire station on a holiday, visiting a nursing home, having neighbors over for dinner, driving an elderly neighbor to the doctor's, picking up the neighbor's mail when they're on vacation; to more grand gestures, like serving on a mission trip or organizing a community fundraiser for a good cause. I once knew a homeless woman near my neighborhood who I made friends with and tried to help any way I could. Homelessness was a choice for her, so she wasn't interested in changing her situation, and she had almost nothing to her name. But she somehow found her way to a

local church every Sunday and volunteered in several capacities. She had a heart for serving and almost nothing to give but her time, which she freely gave.

2. **Appeal to your child's interests.** Volunteering can be mutually beneficial to the giver and the receiver. In Jessica's case, she wanted experience caring for and training dogs, so the SPCA was a good fit for her. She got something she wanted and needed from it, as well as filling a need in the organization as well. There's nothing wrong with volunteering in a place that broadens your child's skills in an area of interest. In fact, if they are interested in a particular thing, they are more likely to enjoy the volunteer experience.

3. **Make it a social activity.** Kids, especially teens, often respond better to volunteer situations when they have some friends doing the same thing. Once when my twins were teenagers, we volunteered with their church youth group to feed the homeless on Thanksgiving through a local organization. We drove to the facility together in a school bus, which was a fun time for the kids. They divvied up jobs and responsibilities among themselves, quickly establishing "dibs" on this job or that. Some worked together on the serving line, some in the dishwashing room and some bussing tables and filling drinks. They laughed at each other wearing hair coverings, aprons, and plastic gloves, joked about scraping plates and washing dishes, but still worked hard to serve those with so much less than themselves. It was an altogether better experience because their friends were there serving in the same capacity.

4. **Present opportunities but give them ownership in choosing.** Often, children want to make a difference in their worlds, but they don't know where to start. Adults can assist children in finding opportunities by doing online searches together, making lists of places to volunteer, and initiating contact with organizations. But the child should have a

say in the final decision based on their likes and dislikes. Having this "ownership" in the process will help ensure that the child is volunteering because he or she wants to and thinks it will be a valuable experience.

5. **Teach them empathy.** Often, empathy is the basis for serving. Empathy is defined as the ability to understand and share the feelings of another. This requires looking at things from different perspectives, which adults can encourage children to do, especially by talking through different situations. In the "Things to Think About" section of this book, I encourage kids to talk to military children to see how their experiences differ from someone growing up consistently in the same house, town, or school. Understanding this different perspective and projecting how it would make you feel to always be moving around, increases a child's awareness that not every child has the same experiences.

6. **Nurturing a caring attitude.** At first, I thought this suggestion was the same as empathy, but then I realized that it's a little broader. A caring attitude for others involves looking beyond oneself as the center of the universe, so to speak. It involves becoming aware that not everyone has food on the table at night, that some people don't have adequate shelter, that animals and children are sometimes mistreated, that the world is full of people and animals in need of help who can't stand up for themselves. Adults can help children practice a caring attitude every day by simple things like teaching children to share, to take turns, and even give up a turn if necessary. Teach them to take care of the things they're given, or of other's things, as a way of showing respect and gratitude for those things. Many simple things can begin to lay the groundwork for an overall caring attitude.

7. **Acknowledge their work.** Children should be praised and even rewarded for their volunteer time. At the SPCA, Jessica got to put a sticker on her name badge for every training she completed. After a

certain amount of time or hours, volunteers were awarded with a puppy paw print pin to put on the name badge. Those are great motivators and make the volunteer feel appreciated and valuable. Adults can certainly reinforce the acknowledgement with simple things like praising the child in front of family and friends for their efforts; maybe printing up a little homemade certificate for every 10 hours completed or offering a small "prize" like a small figure of a dog or a stuffed animal for more hours volunteered. Adults get praised and rewarded for their work (even if it's just a paycheck), and children should, too. One thing Jessica and I did at the SPCA was attend their annual volunteer appreciation dinner and awards night. Jessica didn't get any special awards because her hours were so few compared to so many of the volunteers, but she was treated to an awesome potluck dinner and felt proud being included in the event and part of a great volunteer team.

One of my favorite quotes of all time, by Ralph Waldo Emerson, highlights my feelings about living one's life with purpose. I hope it inspires you and the children you love or influence to make a difference in the world!

> *"The purpose of life is not [just] to be happy. It is to be useful, to be honorable, to be compassionate, to have it make some difference that you have lived and lived well."*

A NOTE ABOUT ADOPTING A PET

Adopting a pet from the SPCA (or any shelter) is always fun and exciting, but please realize that, in the case of a dog or cat, this relationship can last 15 or more years. It's not something to be entered into without the proper forethought and planning. Of course, a goal of the SPCA, in addition to adopting out as many animals as possible, is to reduce the number of animals surrendered to shelters in the first place. They try to ensure this by carefully matching pets with the right family and home situations through their highly trained adoption counselors, and by caring for and preparing the animals for family life as best as they can. Except for animals who come to the shelter from abusive situations, one of the most heartbreaking things is to see an animal returned not long after being adopted, because the family adopted the animal on impulse without carefully considering the impact that pet will have on the family, the home, and the finances. Please teach your children that owning a pet is a big and important responsibility that lasts a long time, before you take them on a trip to the shelter to see and fall in love with a pet.

ABOUT THE AUTHOR

LIZ CIUFO is a former US Army paratrooper and US Army combat veteran of the Persian Gulf War (Desert Shield and Desert Storm) from August 1990—April of 1991, where she served with the XVIII Airborne Corps as an Intelligence Officer. She served six years of active duty in the US Army, four years in the US Army Reserve and thirteen years in the US Air Force Reserve, retiring as a Major in 2005. Elizabeth also holds a Master of Arts degree in Education and is a former middle school teacher.

During that time, Liz married a US Air Force officer and pilot and traipsed around the country with him and later, their two children (twins), for 24 years, homeschooling the twins, taking care of many airmen and their families, and being involved in numerous airmen and military family-oriented agencies and programs.

After retirement, Liz lived on a small hobby farm in northern California for a number of years, growing fruits, vegetables, and herbs, canning and preserving food, and raising sheep and chickens. She now lives with her young adult children (and Cody!) in Las Vegas where she spends her time reading, writing, meeting with old friends who pass through town, and seeing the sights.

Jessica's Dog, Cody, is Liz's third published work, and second in a series of children's books with the theme, "Kids Can Make a Difference!" The first children's book in that series is *Skip's Dog, Lola*. Her other published work is a non-fiction book which is a memoir of her time in Desert Storm called, *A Shoe in the Sand – A Look Behind for the Journey Ahead*. All are available on Amazon. Find Liz on the web at www.lizciufo.com and on Facebook at Liz Ciufo Author.

THINGS TO THINK ABOUT

1. Jessica's father was in the military and she moved nine times in 15 years. Do you know any military children who have moved around a lot in their lives? What do you think it would be like to move every couple of years? Exciting? Difficult? Sad? Fun? List some good and bad things about moving so often. If you know a military child, ask them what it's like to move all the time.

2. Jessica and her twin brother, Joshua, were home schooled and because of that had more flexibility in their school schedule and their lives. This allowed them to travel with their family more, as well as to work and volunteer at a younger age. Are you home schooled, or do you know any children who are home schooled? Talk about what you think would be good about going to school at home, and what you would not like about going to school at home. If you are not home schooled, but know a home schooler, ask them what they like and dislike about doing school that way.

3. Had you ever heard of the SPCA before reading this book? Look up more information about them online and check to see if you have a local SPCA in your town. If you do have one in your town, consider visiting it to see the animals up for adoption, and to watch the staff and volunteers in action. Look to see if there are other animal rescue organizations in your town as well.

4. Have you ever gotten to play with puppies?! What do you think the best thing would be about playing with brand new puppies? Why do you think Jessica fell in love with Cody and not with Sophie? Do you have an animal at home that you dearly love? If so, what do you love about them?

5. Have you read the other book in this series, *Skip's Dog, Lola*? If you did, you would know that in that story, Jessica fell in love with a tiger-striped Boxer named Lola but didn't get to keep Lola. In this book, Jessica gets to keep Cody and take him home as her very own dog. How do you think Jessica felt when her mom said they could adopt Cody and take him home? How would YOU feel if you were getting a new puppy or another animal to take home and love?

6. Do you believe that no matter how young they are, kids can make a difference? If so, what are some ways you think you can make a difference in your home, family, school, or town? Even though you can't volunteer at the SPCA until you're 13 years old there are many younger children who make a difference there. Some collect donations of blankets, towels, and toys from their friends to donate to the SPCA. Some make special cat toys to donate. Some ask for money donations instead of birthday gifts to donate to the SPCA. Make a list of some ways you could help a charitable organization like the SPCA. You could start by asking the organization what kinds of things they most need.

www.ingramcontent.com/pod-product-compliance
Lightning Source LLC
Chambersburg PA
CBHW042355070526
44585CB00028B/2937